The Cup That Heals

- C M BAILEY -

An environmentally friendly book printed and bound in England by www.printondemand-worldwide.com

This book is made entirely of chain-of-custody materials

www.fast-print.net/store.php

The Cup That Heals

ISBN 978-178035-286-2

First published 2012 by
FASTPRINT PUBLISHING
Peterborough, England.
Printed by Printondemand-Worldwide

Preface

In my story there are dramtic accounts of very unusual spiritual happenings. I can understand and expect there will be those who are sceptical, but we must refer to truth in the Bible. We know that Moses ascended Mount Sinai alone and was delivered the Holy Law by God – with no extras around.

When Abraham obeyed God and took his son Isaac to the Land of Moriah for a sacrifice to God he was alone. The sacrifice of Isaac was spared by the miraculous appearance of a ram caught in a thicket. In the New Testament we read and know of the Annunciation of Our Lady. So amazing! Some of the wonder and majesty of the event tends to be lost by the frequent telling. Then there is the story of Nicodemus who visited Jesus by night – no doubt welcoming the cloak of darkness so that his fellow Pharisees would not know what he was up to! The sublime conversion that followed the meeting is a 'jewel' in the Authorised Version.

None of these events were witnessed by a third person; they were uncorroborated yet unquestioned. Nothing has changed; contact is being made, and is, as I have found – one to one – as of old.

The Lord finds and touches people when they are alone.

I have learned a simple lesson from my study of the Bible, and one word sums it up; *obedience.* We are consistently being encouraged to be obedient to the will of God.

The Early Years

It was Easter Day and I was on duty on the children's surgical ward at my General Training School in Leicester, The Royal Infirmary.

Sister had asked me to help her prepare a tiny baby for the mortuary. I was still very early in my general training, in fact in my first year of four.

The tiny baby had died undiagnosed and was to have a post-mortem examination. This necessitated bandaging the little body onto a padded wooden cross. Considering what day it was, this caused me indescribable sadness. Having almost completed the task, Sister suddenly hurried away.

She was soon back, holding a daffodil which she gently tucked between the layers on the tiny breast.

I realised with an overwhelming feeling that this tiny scrap of only four days old was of profound worth, precious, and mattered.

I was feeling somewhat saddened before this as my brother Sam was amongst those on a thousand bomber raid on Berlin. He did not come back.

The baby was four days old, my brother just short of 21 years, so they had both gone very young. But not quite, as I was to learn in incidents of a spiritual nature which proved that we are not lost; our imprint goes on.

I was born in an idyllic village on the edge of the Fawsley Estate, which had been in the hands of the Knightleys for hundreds of years.

The relationship between the "big house" and the villagers was kindly and generous.

We were allowed access to the parkland, woods and lakes. The men fished in the lakes, bold young lads swam naked in the lakes in the summertime and we gathered firewood and picnicked in the park. It was also ideally suited as a venue for the Pytchley Hunt. The relationship was happy in every way - sadly vanished as the "big house" is now a restaurant!

My much-loved grandfather would rattle my bedroom window at about 5 o'clock on summer mornings to rouse me. Off we would go on our bikes into this noiseless world! All that destroyed the peace was animal noise and the crowing of roosters.

We pedalled through the woods and parklands into this magical place.

The grass gleamed, heavily dew-laden, and mist hung over the lakes, gently lifting as the sun warmed. Rabbits tore about in their hundreds while deer and sheep munched away.

Not a soul moved in the "big house" and I would be transfixed by the activity of all those rabbits.

As I reflect now on those times of viewing the simplest of nature's bounty, I wondered: did my grandfather want to inculcate in me the love of nature that motivated him?

In those days people lived closer to the earth and tended it with care, knowing it was that earth from where everything that man has comes. There was a tangible dependence on the earth, the elements and all God's mercies.

For all his Godly ways, my grandfather never went to church; he would sit in the porch and wait for us.

I often wondered why, and found it puzzling.

When he died I was away and unable to be at his funeral, but he had said, When I die, if you are going to a ball, don't put it off just because I have died, I wouldn't want to spoil anything for you!"

I would remonstrate in vain; he was such a dear man.

My step-mother told me that as his coffin was being carried into the church, there was a sudden halt as flowers on top of it were swept off and onto the stone slabs of the nave. It was very unnerving for all present. Perhaps he really did not want to be taken into the church - blaming God for taking loved ones from him.

His only child, my mother, died aged 35 years and Sam, his grandson at just less than 21.

My father had volunteered for service in the 1914-18 war to be with his elder brother John.

John was 18 and my father 16; it would seem that recruiting officers were not too troubled by age discrepancies, two brothers allegedly 18 years old!

My father's service is remarkable for two reasons. In all he received four bullets on different occasions and in different body parts, but the fourth bullet passed through his chest narrowly missing vital organs. The result of his experience in the trenches rendered him a lifelong fatalist. He believed our lives to be mapped out for us.

The other somewhat unique event took place when he was home on "furlough" and he was very disturbed at the extremely frail state of his mother.

His 50 year old father had already died following a fishing holiday; he had pneumonia and his emaciated state meant he had no resistance.

Food was not rationed in that war and yet people did starve.

My shrewd Scots granny survived by sending to Aberdeen for barrels of salted herring.

My father, angered beyond words, took his gun and visited the butcher. The butcher was told if he didn't allow his mother meat, he would be shot. My father threatened him and said

"I may as well be shot for shooting you here, as going back to the trenches to be shot there."

When hostilities ceased and he arrived back home, both his parents had died aged 50 years, his home had been sold and, like thousands of others, he had nothing.

During his absence, his older sister had married and gone to live up north, having sold the home lock, stock and barrel.

My father had been born into a respected middle-class family and now he had nothing save a limp, a facial injury, scars and his medals.

He took lodgings in the tiny village of Eydon and must have been desperately lonely until he met Becky, who he later married. Becky was the only child of a Scottish mother and Midland father and was deeply treasured.

She was the first child in the village to own a bicycle, rather bold in those days.

I was to learn that Becky was brought into the world by a young doctor new to the area; in fact Becky was the first baby to be delivered since his arrival.

The result of this was a special relationship, and Christian names were always used.

A few years passed and I realised that all was not well with my mother and that there would be fairly frequent visits from the doctor and my North Country aunt, a trained nurse.

Granny would take my mother to the seaside to convalesce, and life would return to normal when my mother recovered her health.

One day, as I stood warming myself by the kitchen fire, I heard my father and the doctor coming downstairs, talking quietly.

I was unnoticed as they came into the kitchen, and the doctor was saying "I'm afraid Becky won't make old bones, Arthur."

I wondered what on earth he could possibly mean; they were talking in low tones, so I heard no more. Old bones, old bones, it all seemed very strange and very worrying to my young ears. I couldn't trouble my father as he looked very worried and anxious, but at night time when I awoke I would steal out of my bedroom, go across to theirs and listen by my mother's bedside to hear her breathing and reassure myself that she was all right. No one ever knew of these nocturnal visits and I never told anyone.

The time came when Becky had to go into hospital and stay. It was dreadful for us all, but, as usual, my North Country aunt came down to take charge.

Visiting in hospital was very restricted in those days; one hour only on Wednesday, Saturday and Sunday, so the time spent was very precious. Only two of us could go on any one day.

By a strange coincidence my older cousin was working on Knightly ward as a student nurse. My mother was much alarmed at the amount of work expected of these nurses and said, "No daughter of mine will be a slave!" Circumstances alter cases and it was as well that she didn't know that I was to become a "slave"!

Despite all the efforts of the hospital staff my mother did not improve but, to our unconfined joy, we learnt she would be coming home.

We were less ecstatic when we realised that she was not better and would be going to Granny's house to be quieter, and where there was more room.

Our North Country aunt had taken over charge once more and there was much friction between my aunt and Granny. They did not like each other and vied for supremacy.

The dreadful end came on December 21st. My mother had always delighted in Christmas; it was very special. My father decided she would be with us this very last time.

We went to Granny's house each evening to visit her. She lay in an open coffin on trestles, windows covered and candles flickering.

Her stillness and unsmiling face were difficult for our young minds to understand, she seemed so far away from us. The decision of our father to take us to see her could not have been easy. The result for me was sudden claustrophobia which I didn't understand, fear, feeling ill and not knowing why and no one to tell - how frightening it all was. I have not lost the sudden claustrophobia which will sweep over me unannounced!

The funeral was arranged for Boxing Day, which dawned grey and foggy.

Soon after noon we were all dressed in deepest mourning and Sam got into terrible trouble. He was the oldest of the family, 14 years old and I felt very sorry for him. When ordering his suit of mourning he decided to have link buttons on his single-breasted jacket and a cross-over waistcoat underneath. My father thought this distasteful and inappropriate for Sam to wear at his mother's funeral. But the church bell was tolling and we saw the horse-drawn hearse approaching, so we all left for Granny's house.

The hearse stood under the dripping chestnut trees. My aunt lined us up. I walked with my grieving father.

There was the fog, the heavy scent of flowers and a strange silence in the village. There was no movement, no dog barked and all windows were curtained. There was the clip-clop of the horses and the rumbling of the wheels. This was my mother's funeral, and for everyone else it was Christmas.

By the strange selectivity of the mind, I remember setting off, gripping my father's hand, then nothing else of the church service until, going down the sloping lane towards the cemetery, the horses' hooves began to slip, which worried me. So much is a blur - for which I should perhaps be thankful.

Growing Up Fast

My granny had apprenticed my mother to be a court dressmaker, so she had made her own wedding gown. On the morning of the wedding, being a true country girl, she had gathered bluebells from the woods to be her wedding bouquet. She never wore jewellery, but would pin a flower to her bodice.

During the signing of the register, unbelievably, the priest knocked over the inkwell, spilling ink down my mother's matchless dress.

There were those in the village that deemed that to be an ill-omen, and so it proved to be.

After a couple of sorrowful years, my father began to brighten up - he had met someone!

The lady concerned was Pearl, in many ways not unlike Becky – but she had never been a mother, and there is a difference!

They married, and it meant the departure of Sam and Don to live with Granny! I was considered a traitor as I stayed at home.

Naturally, it made life difficult for us all. My mother, during some of my last moments with her, made me promise never to leave my father.

This I did promise, but future events proved difficult.

It became apparent to me that I was moving on! It seemed that my stepmother, with the connivance of her sister, had arranged an interview for me at an Orthopaedic hospital where they took students at age 17 years.

I was on a hiding to nothing, as three of my aunts and all my cousins were either trained nurses or nurses in training.

It was a desperate time for me as I had had to lose my scholarship at the local grammar school before taking the school certificate. So I had to sit an entrance exam before being accepted as a student. I felt very humiliated. As well as that, with my incomplete education, I felt gauche, naive with the bucolic air of a country bumpkin!

Sam had already volunteered for the RAF so the bond between us, in a way, strengthened.

He was sent off toSaint Athan;, South Wales and then on to Cardington in Bedfordshire and finally to Bomber Command in Lincolnshire.

I was in no way prepared for what I had to face in Orthopaedics, the hospital and staff accommodation was like Lowood in Jane Eyre! My parents had had to buy this mass of voluminous uniform and starched "this and that"! Black stockings and shoes and a butterfly cap! I felt an absolute fright, uniform nearly down to my toes.

Before I left home, my father assured me that he wouldn't be worried about me, as I would soon be back home.

"What makes you say that?", I asked innocently.

"Because you won't be able to keep your tongue between your teeth", he said. Well, we would see.

Time passed quickly, and it wasn't long before I was on a large ward consisting of military personnel and civilians. There were two Sisters, the senior one an absolute dragon, and I thought the junior one daft! No doubt she thought the same of me! One day, by an exquisite piece of timing, as I walked down the main corridor, an arm shot out from a dressing room and I was pulled inside by the "daft" Sister.

She pulled my cap off - as she no doubt decided I was showing too much hair and plonked it back on just above my eyebrows!

I felt, and must have looked, ridiculous. She fixed my cap with dozens of clips and I made my escape towards the ward kitchen.

I didn't realise that she was not far behind me. My grinning colleagues said it all and I said, "The old bitch!", not knowing that "the old bitch" was behind me! Most likely waiting for my reaction. I remember little of what transpired; sufficient to say my father would have been amazed at my servility.

I didn't tell him, as I now knew I had much to learn about discipline and servility.

I learned a lot from this busy "complex", but was thankful when I was moved to theatre, where the Sister was a delight.

She was young, pretty and fun-loving. One day she sat me down by the operating table and, under the arc-light, mowed my eyebrows with pair of dissecting forceps. Having acquired a lipstick and a bra, I began to look less like a country bumpkin.

When my next off-duty came, it coincided with a weekend when I knew Sam would be home - so I was excited at the very thought.

I went up to Granny's house to see them all and meet Sam again and I was very bold.

Granny toddled off to make us all some cocoa. There was absolutely no choice at that time, so as she went I dived into my handbag. I had a special surprise in there for Sam, and I produced my cigarette case. Sam was so astonished that he spilt his cocoa down his uniform! I proceeded to light both our cigarettes as my grandfather tittered behind his newspaper. I was waiting for Granny to blow a gasket, but she proved to be a real sport, and said not a word.

When I returned to duty I crowned myself with glory, I would imagine - the only time in my life. We had a heavy theatre list, and I was the general dogsbody, that is, I was not "scrubbedup" wearing sterile gowns, but was responsible for everything running smoothly.

All was going well, we had a middle-aged man on the table who had suffered a tubercular spine, now quiescent, and was having surgery to remove diseased bone and to reinforce and arthrodese the spine with a graft from the tibia.

There was a sudden abrupt halt to the soft purring of the electric saw being used to take the leg graft. All eyes were on me, as there was not another saw sterile, that is, usable!

In those brief moments I wondered what they expected of this lowest of the low in the profession? I calmly took my scissors from my pocket, switched off the current, very deftly isolated the errant wire and replaced it.

It was all sorted out in moments, the sterile clothes removed from the operation site, and an audible sigh of relief pervaded the place. I was just doing what I was there for and saved the day - but I had learnt nothing of electricity in the lecture room. No, this was a snippet taught us by the headmaster of the little village school that I first attended. How prescient he was!

As a result of this episode I began to feel less "at the bottom of the heap", especially as the eminent surgeon concerned would stop me and have a little chat thereafter when we met.

I grasped the opportunities presented to me and got stuck into my studies. I had a rabid appetite for it all.

My moral education was somewhat challenged, much to my surprise, at this select establishment where I thought I was moving amongst young ladies.

One quite insignificant looking girl displayed a surprising hidden talent whilst on night duty on a male ward. One of the night Sisters had done the midnight round and left the men's ward to carry on to the children's block. For some strange, uncanny reason, she doubled back and revisited the men's ward. The night nurse was not in the office or the wards, so Sister checked a large dressing room. She flung the door open to find the "insignificant" night nurse in bed with a patient. The patient was in the dressing room for special observation as he had had spinal surgery and was in a Thomas' bedframe.

It would appear that the nurse took the "special observation" rather seriously and got a bit too close!

When we all went in to Night Nurses' breakfast that morning, the Sisters were tight-lipped.

The bush telegraph soon told us what had happened and by the time day staff arrived on duty she had gone lock, stock and barrel. During the night the Sisters had cleared her room and arranged for her to be taken home, never to be seen again. It would be interesting to know what she told her parents!

My night duty was on a women's ward and I was concerned about one of my post-op patients who was not sleeping well, so I asked night Sister if she would check a sedative for her in case she didn't sleep that night.

During the very small hours the lady woke. I went through the usual procedure of making her comfortable and giving her a warm drink and she was soon asleep.

I had looked at the checked sedative, cogitated about giving it to her, and on balance decided against.

When I arrived on duty the next night Day Sister was waiting for me. I inwardly groaned: what had I done, or not done, I thought, what a wonderful start for the night!

She said, "Well, nurse, you have had a narrow escape! When you had just gone off duty, the senior pharmacist came tearing up the ward in a great panic. It seems that, unnoticed by anyone, the undiluted stock bottle of the sedative was sent to the ward in error. If you had given the checked dose to your patient you would have killed her! I felt weak at the knees and could only think all the angels in Heaven were looking after us that night. There would have to have been an inquest with me in the thick of it, having innocently given a lethal dose!

There was a traumatic night for me soon after this when night Sister helped me to perform the last offices on a young girl, Norma. She had been a pretty 15 year old and had spent the last two years of her life immobilised in a splint in an effort to try and overcome the devastating action of the tubercle bacillus eating away at her spine.

The last offices were a very precise discipline carried out with much reverence for the deceased.

I was very moved and saddened by the death of Norma at such a tender age. Her life had been short and painful and I could only think that her death could not have been in vain, as she was spotless. She was a sweet child, still remembered as I write about her, would that we all could be as blameless.

We can only be thankful that the crippling surgical tuberculosis, spread, it is thought, by badgers, is more or less eradicated. We must be thankful for the TB testing of cattle to keep our milk safe.

I was put in a compromising position one Sunday morning. I had now passed my state and hospital Finals for my Orthopaedic Certificate, so they thought me capable of being left in charge of the military wing.

Several of the convalescent soldiers had applied for, and been granted, church passes.

The "church" they had been to, I was to learn later, was the local pub.

Matron, from her "eyrie" at the front of the main building, had obviously been alerted to the "rag tag and bobtail" sauntering down the drive, and unknown to me she decided to follow them.

I was in the main corridor as they stumbled in, swooped on me and tossed me up in the air again and again and again.

I was helpless and suddenly and ignominiously dropped on the stone floor.

Matron stood in the large entrance, obviously not disappointed in what she beheld.

The patients, needless to say, melted away.

I had to pick myself up and face her. I was given no chance to defend myself and was treated with condemnatory scorn. We did the ward round in total silence; she found nothing to criticise!

The undeserved ignominy I was made to suffer brought me lasting wisdom; I had won the gold medal but the glory of an ounce of gold was soon dissipated.

Apart from the medical mountain I had to climb, I needed knowledge of devious and calculating behaviour that I had not met in my childhood. I had to learn that not all people are nice!

I had been robbed of what little I had, denigrated and hurtfully treated during those years of orthopaedic training, but in the process

I had acquired some wisdom and defensive armoury.

My father had been born into a much respected lower middle class family, but along with thousands of others he lost everything when he returned to the "home" he no longer had, at the age of twenty.

I was entered into the nursing profession' which at that time was snob-ridden. I was one of the have-nots. The humiliation and hateful practice I contended with I never spoke of to my father. Only those who have endured this treatment will know what I am talking about. The lesson I learnt was a lifetime's loathing of snobbery.

I Move On!

I moved on from orthopaedics, intending to take a comprehensive General Nurse Training for State Registration. With my orthopaedic qualifications and gold medal I was deemed acceptable for general training at Leicester Royal Infirmary. I had to sign on for four years, with the qualification that if I married during that time I would be fined and dismissed.

A friend of mine fell in love with an American Serviceman, married and paid the full penalty.

Although quite experienced by now, I found the wards at this very busy acute hospital terrifying. The Nightingale wards were frighteningly large, having as many as 60 patients on some of them. They were kept in immaculate, disciplined order by the Sisters, paragons in grey! How unruffled they seemed alongside all this serious illness!

Would I ever be one of them? A distant dream. Mercifully, we were let down lightly and gradually introduced to the wards from the training school.

The transition for me was as from Hades to Heaven. Despite the drama and the trauma apparent everywhere, the place ticked over like clockwork and we were as one enormous family. The people were nice.

At the end of preliminary training, we all had a short time off and were allowed to go home.

It was with great delight that I scuttled off to catch the train. I knew Sam wouldn't be home; he had been posted to Bomber Command and was on the thousand bomber raids.

The last time we had all been together, Sam had talked to Dad about what he was doing. It left my father very thoughtful. Sam had agreed it was very dangerous. He said, "Three of us are mates, one is an only child, the other the father of twins, and there is me. None of us wants to die."

When I arrived at the little station three miles from home I faced a long, lonely walk. I always felt somewhat nervous as we knew tramps slept in the hedge bottoms as they travelled between Banbury and Daventry workhouses.

I had barely started my walk when it began to snow and a wind sprang up. I took off the scarf round my neck and pinned it over my hair with my R.A.F. broach redolent of Sam. I carefully fastened the safety clip on my brooch and carried on with my walk.

The snow fell more heavily as the wind strengthened and I was very glad to see the faint glimmer of the village, despite wartime restrictions.

Reaching home, I knocked the snow off my boots at the back door and was thankful to feel the warmth and glow of the kitchen.

My step-mother and two young siblings were at home.

Once in, I reached up to unpin my scarf, but the brooch wasn't there - it had gone.

My scarf was still in place, as I had put it, not knotted, despite high wind and snow.

How could this possibly be? I was disturbed by this somewhat bizarre happening. I was troubled.

This kind of thing could not happen. My brooch had gone, but where and how I didn't know.

Anyway, I was home and there was much to talk about. Soon my young siblings were off to bed and my step-mum and I could have a long chat.

I suddenly realised, now that we were alone, that Pearl looked very solemn and serious.

What was all this about?

She had something to tell me, she said, and they had decided it was kinder to tell me when I was home rather than over the phone. Bluntly, Sam was missing.

My father had received the starkly formal note from the Air Ministry to say that his plane had failed to return from a Thousand Bomber raid on Berlin.

He never came back.

As Pearl was speaking, I was hardly listening as my mind had leapt back to the missing R.A.F. brooch and its link with Sam.

The only explanation possible is that by some extraordinary means he had been with me at some time during my lonely walk. How did he know that I was on my way home? He would not have wanted Pearl to be the one to tell me that he was no longer with us.

We had said our good-byes at the little station about a month before. Sam had gone off to Lincolnshire and my train a little later to Leicester.

We said our cheery good-byes and were not to meet again.

On the back of the last photo of him, he wrote his own epitaph.

I shall pass through this world but once

Any good deed that I can do for any fellow creature

Let me do it now.

Let me not defer it, or neglect

For I shall not pass this way again.

I have pondered, over the years, how Sam knew that I was going home, walking alone, not having been told that he had died?

I was to be graphically shown that those we have loved and who have gone from us are nevertheless very much alive. I have been left in no doubt that we are known and often guided by those we have loved.

During my time of training in general nursing, we had no intensive wards; the intensive nursing was carried out in side wards.

The corner beds were reserved for the very ill and people knew that anyone occupying them would be going only one way.

All sorts of emergencies arrived on these very busy wards at all hours of the day and night. No waiting on trolleys in those days, patients were quickly whisked up to the wards.

Some patients, for indefinable reasons, remain fixed in the memory.

One young man arrived in a very distressed condition one morning. He was the only son of a farmer, and obviously exempt from military service.

The farmer had a much cherished prize bull. On this day, the unbelievable happened. The bull, enraged, chased and tossed the youth.

In so doing, by some bizarre chance, the boy's entire genitalia was sliced off.

The parts were not found! Caring for him was excruciatingly difficult and any treatment most delicate. We were all about his age. He eventually was transferred from us to receive plastic surgery.

In his case avoidance of military service possibly did him no favours.

The mind of the farmer's son would have been much affected by the tragic incident, as was the mind of a mystery patient, again a comparatively young man, again excused call-up.

I learned much about the control the mind has over the body, but not in the lecture room.

The patient concerned was a good-looking young man who had become paralysed from the waist down. He was married, had a job and his wife was pregnant.

He was barrier-nursed as the cause of the paralysis was unknown and polio had to be excluded by multiple tests.

Every test came back from the lab negative and the situation was boringly normal - apart from the continued paralysis. His wife visited regularly and they seemed happy.

Eventually physiotherapy was brought into play and two therapists would get him up on crutches. Progress was almost nil, but he was able eventually to manage "elbow sticks".

The "up patients" enjoyed a few privileges such as helping with the after-dinner drinks. David liked to join in with this and would hang onto the back of the large, cumbersome trolley and be pushed along and feel that he was doing his bit.

One day, going off to dinner, I met one of my colleagues and had a brief chat. She was working on the maternity block. She remarked that they had admitted a mother whose husband was on my ward. I asked if all was going well with the labour and was assured that everything was fine.

When I arrived back at my ward, the merry band of helpers was in the kitchen, clearing the drinks trolley for the kitchen staff, David among them. I spotted David and said that I had some wonderful news for him: his wife had been admitted to have the baby.

I got no further, as with a dreadful clatter David crashed to the floor, helpless.

I quickly rang for two porters to get David onto a trolley and into bed. His paralysis was again complete and entire.

What a fool I felt, and an idiot. Had I been a better nurse, I would have sat him down before imparting important news for him.

I had much to learn before I could consider myself a decent nurse.

David had instantly resumed total loss of power to his lower limbs on hearing that his wife was in hospital. I had acted stupidly, but we had our diagnosis: his trouble was an exaggerated fear and hysteria for his wife's safety during her pregnancy.

The fear had produced a phantom paralysis quite beyond his control. Each time his wife had visited he had fed on his fear.

Once she was safely delivered, David's recovery was rapid and complete.

I have learnt much about the disabling effect of worry and anxiety on the body.

An easy way to understand what had happened to David is to think about a rape victim.

If a person is grabbed off the street and subjected to rape, one would expect to hear loud screams.

The effort to shout and scream can be completely ineffective. Throat muscles become constricted and no sound comes out from the terrified individual.

The victim is incapacitated because the usually protective mind has failed to allow the screams.

The obscure subtlety of the mind has gone into over-drive, willing the patient to give in to prevent fatal damage by screaming. The protective mind really is a best friend.

The Rainbow

I succumbed to a severe viral infection that attacked my lungs, making me feel very ill. The usual medication proved useless, and as I coughed away day and night, I began to despair. My doctor was not very helpful and I gained the impression that he thought I was "swinging the lead".

After visiting me at home, he told me to get back on duty and forget it. Weeks of coughing had left me feeling very weak and tired. I put my uniform on nevertheless and knew that I was quite incapable of looking after others as I was.

So back I went to bed.

The next morning, the sun was shining behind the curtains, and the rush-hour traffic was tearing by. I felt abandoned and alone with this dreadful problem, in fact I felt I might die.

Suddenly my attention was drawn to the window, and above it to the pelmet. As I watched with incredulous fascination, very slowly a rainbow materialised and hung there.

It was perfect in every way, filling the space across the window width, caught in a gentle mist. Hardly daring to breathe, I wondered what on earth it meant.

As I watched, gradually, barely perceptibly, it began to fade and vanish.

I lay in my bed never having witnessed anything like it, and more or less mechanically picked up my Bible from the bedside table.

As I opened it, thinking of the intriguing happening of moments earlier, my eyes rested on words that sprang from the page at me.

"I will put my bow in the cloud as a sign of my covenant with you." Genesis chapter 9 verse 13

The full impact of what had happened to me began to dawn.

I had to accept that my ill-condition was known and that I had been targeted.

How was it possible? I felt a sense of shock and fear; fear to think of how we are known. I remembered the strangely comforting words of God: "Before you were born, I knew you."

Jesus spoke of separating the sheep from the goats, and I felt very much one of the goats, hard to convince. I felt unworthy and too ashamed, almost, to believe what had happened. Anyway, it had, and suddenly I felt energised, strengthened and very bold.

I dressed, fetched my scooter from the garage and sailed up to the surgery.

A doctor was there and I said I wished to see a consultant, privately and quickly; he looked slightly taken aback!

I soon saw an eminent physician and was very thoroughly examined. I had X-rays, E.C.G., blood tests and more.

At the end of all that, the delightful man sat me down as I waited with a heavy heart for his diagnosis. When it came, I had another shock. Why on earth had my doctor not realised my problem? But then, he hadn't put his stethoscope on my chest. Not once!

I had asthma, he informed me, and quite badly. No wonder I felt ill, I had had untreated asthma for weeks.

"What is more," he said, "you will probably have it for life." I groaned at this, as I had nursed asthma, some very severe cases and I was very frightened of it.

He said, "Your virus has sparked it off" and he added cheerily, "it could happen to anyone, it could happen to me!"

He gave me a month's conventional treatment, after which I should see him for a further X-ray and review. As I rode home I pondered on the recent events, and wondered what would have happened to me, had it not been for the "rainbow".

With the appropriate medication, I soon began to feel better and strengthened. When I got back to work, I had said to myself, "I don't want asthma, I am not going to have asthma, it can go away!" I practised this times a day accompanied by deep-breathing exercises. I soon began to feel much better, returning to normal, for which I thanked God.

The time came for me to revisit the physician. I felt that this was going to be a waste of his time and mine, and so it was!

I had to go through the motions of the re-X-ray and was summoned to the presence.

"Well", he said", much to my surprise, "your X-ray is clear, you won't need to see me again."

I knew that I was back to normal, but he didn't know of the stupefying incident of the rainbow.

The effect of this incident caused me to pull my socks up as now I knew that I was "known"! We have listened to the happenings of two thousand years ago, but that was then; we don't expect such things to happen today, but how wrong we are. The same miraculous events take place and we must all remember that God does keep all his promises to us. Our duty is to be worthy of such truths.

My training was progressing well and by now I was a second-year nurse on a "gynae" ward night duty. One night one of the Sisters turned up to tell me I was wanted to "special" a patient in an isolation ward. I inwardly rebelled, "Why pick me!" I thought. Anyway, I had to leave my ward and "special" a young woman who was extremely ill. I was told to gown-up and put on a mask and gloves as the patient had tetanus.

The young woman was thrashing about in a cot, with the sides up to prevent self-harm. Her arms were restrained each side with bandages and she cut a very sorry figure. Her back was arched, her teeth clenched and I looked at the evil-looking tongue forceps on the locker and prayed I would not need to use them on her.

I was much relieved when my spell of duty was over and I could leave the poor demented creature.

It seems that she had several young children, had been pregnant again and her over-burdened husband had used one of his farming tools to try to secure an abortion.

He wasn't to know that deadly tetanus spores were present on the tool.

The wife died and the husband was in the most dreadful trouble as he was on a charge of manslaughter.

A similar event took place a few days later when I was working in theatres. We were doing a "gynae" list when we were alerted that an emergency was on the way up.

The theatre was quickly re-organised to deal with this. I was in the corridor when the trolley arrived with the patient propped up to assist her breathing as she was heavily pregnant.

She was virtually navy blue and looked desperately anxious and afraid. She was taken straight into theatre with no preliminaries and anaesthetised for a Caesarean section.

Very soon a noisy, active infant was delivered, but by now the mother was dead.

The husband was sent for and the baby placed in his arms. They had several other children. Their mother was taken to the mortuary.

That theatre was closed for the remainder of the day, following custom, out of respect for the grieving family.

How thankful we should be that safe birth control is used today and expectant mothers well cared for.

These experiences reminded me of my own mother who had died so tragically young.

I had done some of my medical lectures and realised that my mother's heart disease was a legacy from the rheumatic fever she had as a young girl of 14 years.

I had remembered Granny telling me that she pushed my mother, as a 14 year old girl, in a spinal carriage when she had this illness. Damage to the heart muscle could be an unfortunate result. My mother, who was ill when I was born, was told to have no more children. She did, and died at 35 years.

I was still on a steep learning curve with endless lectures, mostly taken during our off-duty periods. I have very happy memories of a Sister I worked for on a woman's medical ward. She was a star; we all loved her.

She had an uncle, she told me, a rear gunner in a Halifax bomber during the war. Being the rear gunner he couldn't drop any bombs – but he did his bit. On the way to the plane he would pick up a brick and, once over enemy territory he dropped his brick. It gave him much satisfaction, feeling that he had done some damage.

We had a very glamorous houseman (as all the young doctors were called, male or female, before we became politically correct) blonde, curvaceous; Sister disliked her intensely.

"Look at her!", she would say, "The tart, she's got her breasts slung up with Elastoplast!"

I shuddered as I thought of this embellishment, and marvelled at the uses of Elastoplast. I must say, we rarely saw so much glamour in a white coat.

I was busily doing dressings one afternoon when an emergency arrived, a young woman with severe abdominal pains. Sister called me away from what I was doing to catheterise her.

Other staff members were taking blood and administering oxygen, so I didn't see the girl's face. Despite all our efforts, she died.

A few days later, Sister asked me to go down to the mortuary to identify a body - mentioning the girl's name.

"I can't do it", I said, "I didn't see her face, only her tail."

"That's right" said Sister, "go and identify her."

I grabbed my cloak and set off for the morgue, a horrible job, none of us liked anything to do with the P.M. rooms or the mortuary. It all smelled very heavily of formalin.

The undertakers were already there, and there sat one of the porters on the edge of a coffin, nonchalantly smoking a cigarette. All very informal. I looked at the young face, never previously seen and nodded.

He had said, "Is this her, nursie?" They knew we hated this job, so the smirk on his face was not unexpected. I was glad to make my escape and prayed that the young girl was the one I had catheterised, and that there would be no repercussions.

Sister was doing a ward round when I slipped back in, she saw me and gave me a crafty wink, and that was that.

Among the rows of beds was an attractive young woman; although she was very ill, her personality shone through. We were all fond of her.

She had fairly frequent visits from her brother who was an army officer.

He would strut into the ward, carrying his swagger cane, and ignored all.

One day the balloon went up! He felt his sister was being neglected, not making the progress she should and he demanded to see Sister.

An appointment was made and, as would be expected from such a disciplined character, he turned up bang on time.

He clattered down the corridor and was duly shown into Sister's office.

We were all alerted and expectant of this meeting, and were not disappointed.

The meeting didn't last long, and the young officer turned left from Sister's office and hurried away from the ward.

Sister had given the information he demanded as next of kin. His sister was in the tertiary stages of syphilis and nothing could be done for her.

We never saw the young officer again.

A Break From Nursing

The inevitable happened and, like many nurses, I met and married an ex-patient. Vernon was a member of the police force, and I had no idea what I was letting myself in for. In those days, at the whim of the Chief Constable we could be moved anywhere in two counties. It inevitably meant much loneliness for me and our children as, to begin with, we had four homes in our first five years, miles apart. Wives were not allowed to work, as police property was provided and the wife was an unpaid helper.

Moving us around was necessary as the move generally meant some kind of promotion, but hardly compensated for this kind of itinerant life.

When our two young sons were old enough and accepted into the church choir, we would occasionally leave them and motor on to the tiny village church of Stapleton to take our communion there.

This day everything was proceeding normally and there was nothing to suggest that the day would be in any way different.

We had reached the point where we were proceeding towards the communion rail when I was stopped dead in my tracks.

This day in this tiny church, my life changed forever. The stillness was rocked for me as a soft male voice said to me

"Why do you doubt me?" I knew it was Jesus.

I stiffened, and was then suddenly aware of Vernon giving me a gentle push forward.

Everything was normal, no one else had heard what I heard. There was no scintilla of doubt in my mind, I had been targeted again, and I knelt at the altar rail in tears.

Why was I being targeted? What had I done, or not done? I found it disturbing and upsetting.

Soon after this I was looking through a drawer where there were a few keep-sakes.

I opened a letter from an old patient, a priest, one Grosvenor Jackson, who I remembered very well. When he knew we were to be married, he sent us a present.

Again I wept as I read what he had written, telling me how he had watched me on the ward and how much he loved my Christ-likeness as I went about my duties.

I felt that I had betrayed his thoughts of me; I felt ashamed, a very deep shame.

I realised that I had changed. There was the difficulty of making ends meet as we were very poorly paid until James Callaghan became Home Secretary and almost doubled our pay at a stroke.

We were living in a materialistic world and life was full of difficulties - not least knowing the troubles and sorrows of the community in which we lived.

Nevertheless, drastic steps needed to be taken. I had got to change, revert to how I once was. I needed to pull my socks up.

I started serious re-education by finding time at bed-time to read. I read the Bible from cover to cover, I read the Venerable Bede, Julian of Norwich, Dietrich Bonhoeffer and other theologians. So now I had read all the books! I had, of course, been baptised and confirmed, so now I was a good Christian. I knew deep within myself that I was not yet a good Christian; I needed my L-plates. Having read a book by Albert Schweitzer, I found the very last sentence of his book, "The Quest of the Historical Jesus" a wonderful summary for all of us. He suggests that through all our travails and difficulties as we journey through life we would meet and know the historical Jesus.

Pinchy

When my husband was promoted to Inspector, we were moved into an urban area. He applied for, and was given at last, permission to buy our own house. It meant a degree of freedom, and I could go back into nursing. I had no choice in the matter, as I had to earn the mortgage and our children's higher education was looming.

I would have preferred hospital work, but as my husband worked night duty at times, I wished to avoid that for the sake of the family.

An opportunity arose for a Day Sister's job in an upmarket nursing home which I was lucky enough to secure.

I felt guilty leaving the ordinary folk I had nursed; these people were moneyed, well-travelled, interesting and privileged, but had valid needs too, so I came to terms with the dilemma.

Our only daughter was 14 years of age at the time, and the family at a very interesting stage.

One morning, having fed the children, I was about to leave for work when Isabel had a minor accident. She tripped and fell down the four steps from the top of the staircase onto a small landing. She was shaken up, but appeared alright.

Vernon was already busy on the garden, so I popped down to tell him and suggest that Isabel might need a Panadol. I left it to him to decide if she was fit for school.

After our evening meal, Vernon had resumed his police duties and, as I needed to do some ironing, I took the table into the living room to be with Isabel as she worked on her homework.

As I watched her, I reflected on the morning's happening and thought, "Thank God she didn't hurt herself."

But, I became suddenly aware of something the matter with her spine; it didn't look quite right. She had on a flimsy dress and she said, "I'm all right Mum", to my unasked question, but I wasn't sure. I asked her to let me just check her back. What I saw horrified me, and it wasn't caused by her fall, that I knew for a certainty; no, I saw the start of a scoliosis.

She was shooting up very fast, and I knew my practised eye hadn't deceived me. I tried not to transmit my fear to her, and made light of it. After my years of orthopaedic nursing the picture raced before me. At this time in her scholastic career it couldn't be worse. I knew exactly what it meant; months in hospital and major surgery.

I was still awake when Vernon came off duty at 2am. He assured me that I was wrong and that my imagination was working overtime.

We saw the doctor the next morning and he confirmed my worst fears and said that she must see a consultant.

I had a friend who was an orthopaedic surgeon so I rang him and was invited to take Isabel to his home. Again my fears were confirmed, but he was very kind and gentle with Isabel. He asked if we would like to take her to see a friend of his, a consultant at Harlow Wood, whose speciality was spines.

We were soon speeding up the motorway with Isabel to see this specialist. Isabel was deeply traumatised by all of this and we could offer little comfort to her.

As soon as I saw this now eminent surgeon I remembered having done ward rounds with him years earlier. It made it much more bearable, knowing him.

After examining the X-rays he sat me down to tell me what was what. A five-and-a-half hour operation, bone graft from her hip, nursed on her face in a spinal frame for weeks. He pointed out that the operation needed to be carried out quickly due to Isabel's spurt of growth, or it would get much worse.

She was soon admitted and everything set in motion for her ordeal. Isabel was a wonderful patient and accepted everything with enviable grace.

The hospital had its own school, so she was able to continue her studies. Life for us was hectic as we spent many hours tearing up and down the motorway between duties.

I had a patient at the time who was a loner, strange, a mystic. He was childless, and much concerned that my daughter should have to face such major surgery in her youthful years. He would come down to Sister's office and leave a package on the desk. "The Lord has told me this, the fruit of the vine to make Isabel better." Many bunches of grapes went up the motorway to Isabel from Pinchy. He wasn't a well man by any means and he became terminally ill. He was in the sick bay and was going to die.

One morning I had been to 7am communion before going on duty. After reading night Sister's report I went to visit Pinchy. I told him that I had been to church and had said a little prayer for him.

"I knew you would", he said. "I won't get better, but Isabel will. When she is better, her support will fall off."

"Well", I thought as I left him, "that's not very likely, as her support is welded with steel bolts. Nevertheless, a novel idea."

At work we were not encouraged to take personal telephone calls, so I was somewhat irritated when the secretary informed me that I was wanted on an outside line.

It was my husband ringing to say the Headmaster had rung him. They did not know what to do with Isabel as her support was collapsing, as two bolts had sheared off it!

Vernon knew that I couldn't get off duty, so I suggested that he rang the hospital to alert them to what had happened, and that he was bringing her up right away. It was all resolved painlessly.

The splint department had been alerted and were ready to deal with Isabel on arrival, as she said "banged up again."

The staff were completely mystified by what they found. None of them had ever known one of these bolts to shatter. It was unheard of; they could not believe that it was possible.

Anyway, it had happened, and Isabel was hoping that she would soon be allowed out of the support for brief periods. The drill was, over time she would be allowed out one hour a day, with the time gradually extended over weeks.

It was soon time for review with Mr Jackson and, after a few preliminaries she was taken off for X-ray. Mr Jackson carefully examined the X-rays and looked puzzled. What was to come? We all felt anxious.

What he said will be remembered by Isabel for ever. "Well, your spine is healed; you can come out of that support now."

We thought that he meant for the one hour a day routine, but, no, he said "you can leave that support here, you are completely healed."

Isabel's joy was unconfined. She felt free as a bird; she could wear ordinary clothes and even go to Germany with her colleagues on the planned holiday, not having to wear her supports!

As we crossed the car park, we all looked at each other and chorused,

"How did Pinchy know?"

His words came back to us, "When Isabel is better, her support will fall off."

It is obvious that some spiritual attention had been directed at Isabel and her support!

We were reminded of what St. Paul said about our special gifts, and Pinchy certainly had his!

Isabel's minor accident, falling down four steps, had alerted me to her spinal condition; it was a merciful accident that drew my attention to her.

Polly

Just before coming off duty one day I had to admit a suddenly seriously ill patient to Sick Bay. She had become ill with an infected chest, a condition not helped by the fact that she was somewhat overweight.

She was soon made comfortable, given appropriate treatment and settled down. I was very fond of this delightful lady. One of her major skills was her needlework, particularly crocheting.

Her work was much admired and, knowing that my daughter was also a keen sewer, she had sent Isabel samples of her work. These took the form of medallions of various examples of her work. They were beautiful, and Isabel kept them in their box in a cupboard in the dining room.

On arriving home that evening, I decided I would be blitzing the kitchen after dinner. I was alone in the house, so it was a good opportunity to deal with this task. I worked away for some time and finished off by giving my terrazzo tiles a good scrub. I was quite proud of our very nice kitchen floor; I felt pleased with myself at having got this mundane task out of the way and, as I left the kitchen, I glanced back at it all and took my tools to the utility room.

I wasn't out for long, washed my hands and opened the door. I stood frozen to the spot as, lying on the still-damp kitchen floor was one of Polly's medallions! No one else was in the house, the door to the hall was closed: how on earth had it got there? It was completely inexplicable.

The medallion had travelled out of the cupboard, across the living room, across the hall and through the door into the kitchen! How?

I picked it up, fingered it and eventually returned it to its box in the cupboard, thinking, "How very strange!"

The next morning, on arriving on duty, I followed my usual practice and read Night Sister's report. I received an unpleasant shock: my lovely patient Polly had suddenly collapsed and died during the previous evening. I suddenly felt a chill as I put the two events together. Polly knew I would be very saddened by her death, which I was, so was she trying to communicate with me? There can be no other explanation!

How on earth did she know where I lived, that I would be blitzing my kitchen, and where I kept her medallions in the living room?

Again, I found it all thought-provoking, but this was not in isolation, many similar events were to occur and leave me in no doubt of survival after death.

A Naughty Boy

Two of our patients were not at all well. Jane had a fairly serious heart condition, but her husband was much more complicated.

He had been an army officer serving abroad, and his wife confided in me that during that time he had contracted syphilis. This had occurred fairly early in their married life. They had discussed together what was to be done and they embarked on treatment in Harley Street. She forgave him unhesitatingly and supported him totally. The treatment was long and costly.

I knew from having worked on "special ward" during my training in those pre-penicillin days that the treatment was very harsh and painful. Large-bore intra-muscular needles were necessary to inject the arsenical preparations into the buttocks. Side effects were many and unpleasant.

Nevertheless, at the end of the protracted treatment, our patient was assured that the offending spirochete was exterminated.

Little did they know that the organism was still working and, over time, invading many areas of his body, skin, eyes, kidneys and skeleton. He was a difficult patient, irascible; aside from the pain and many discomforts was the added depression of knowing that all their time, money and effort to eradicate the disease had been in vain.

When he died, his family, who lived in the Middle East, came over for the funeral. The daughter, who now had children of her own, had been left in total ignorance of her father's condition. This was how Jane wanted it. The death certificate had to be collected from the doctor in the surgery, so I duly took her along. Having introduced her, I left them to their discussion. As I closed the door, I heard the doctor say, "I'm afraid that your father has been a naughty boy." I heard no more, but felt very sorry that this news had to be conveyed.

Truth has to be on a death certificate and it could not be hidden. Jane was devastated that her daughter had to hear this dreadful news in this way. The daughter, too, was beyond consoling.

The family returned to the Middle East, but not for very long.

Jane, by now floundering and depressed, began to go rapidly downhill and was in Sick Bay. She needed careful nursing, oxygen from time to time, but appeared not to be quite terminal.

I had been Shanghaied to do a Saturday morning duty, due to staff shortage at holiday time. It was a busy morning and at one stage I stopped off to give out the coffees in Sick Bay, Jane included. We had a few words and she gave no cause for alarm.

Later than usual, due to the hectic morning, I popped back for the empty coffee cups to take to the main kitchen. To my shock and complete astonishment, Jane was no longer with us.

I thought about why she had died so suddenly; with a heart condition, all the shock and involvement with her husband's funeral, her upset at her daughter receiving unpleasant news was all enough to bring on fatal failure.

I went through the usual procedure, rang the doctor who gave me permission to remove the body to the mortuary.

I could have left the last offices to the staff coming on at two o'clock, but felt that I wanted to carry out this last service to Jane myself. I reflected on this brave little woman and her fierce loyalty to her husband, which I felt very admirable.

About a week later, I was passing by what had been Jane's room and felt impelled to go in.

It was still empty.

I wandered over to the window, thought about her and had a general look round. For some strange reason, I felt guided toward the bedside locker. More intensely, I felt that I must look inside it. I stooped to open the door: what on earth did I expect to find? I felt rather stupid. Of course, the locker was empty, but more strongly, I felt that I had to pull the locker out from the wall and look behind. This I did, and there was something lying on the floor. I stooped to pick it up, a bottle, and it was empty. It had Jane's name on it, and it had contained the powerful sedative Nembutal! I realised in an instant what this meant. Jane had it all planned, she would know my moves, that having given her her coffee I would not be around for a while. Time to take the pills and push the empty bottle behind the locker, later to be carelessly swept up by the cleaning ladies!

What was I to do? Not a lot. The family was back in the Middle East and Jane had already been cremated.

I know that I was meant to discover this final subterfuge of Jane's, but how?

There was no realistic reason for me to look behind the locker, nor would I have done so, but for the overwhelming urge to.

Why had I felt the need to go and look around an empty room, moving the locker to look behind it? It all related to Jane's sudden unexpected death.

Is it really true that our friends and loved ones, gone from this life, are so near that they can influence us?

I know that I was propelled towards that locker by a force outside myself.

We hear of musicians such as John Lill, who has stated that he firmly believes the great Beethoven has influenced his career, and there are many others so convinced. It can happen to the great and good, so why not we lesser mortals?

Jane wanted me to know of her final subterfuge, and I can understand why, but how do they manage it? And do they know when their efforts have been successful?

The Old Testament, Again

When incidents occur which cannot be easily explained, they are usually dismissed as fantasy. My feet are firmly planted on the ground, but I have found some incidents difficult to rationalise and come to terms with. I have always avoided such cults as spiritualism, as I think of them as unsettling, but many bereaved people do seem to find comfort from séances with mediums.

However, if the "other-side", parallel world, call it what you will, contacts us? Unsolicited!

I had spent a busy afternoon in the garden, and came into the house to bath and change.

The day had been glorious, and the sun still streamed through the bathroom window. I was standing by the sink, scantily clad, when suddenly I was hit from above and behind by what felt like tiny blocks of ice. This very cold bombardment went on for a few moments, leaving me completely baffled.

I wondered what on earth was happening! I dragged the stool towards the window, examined the pelmet, the light-fitting, looked around, everything was perfectly normal, no sign of anything wet or a leak anywhere.

Again, I was dumbfounded.

Life carried on much as usual, so I had more or less forgotten the incident when “bingo”, two days later a carbon copy of the event occurred.

There had to be an explanation! I had twice been sprinkled with these tiny, ice-cold drips of water, like tiny arrows hitting me. Where had it come from, and what was it all about?

I opened my Bible, as I usually did for a short read before lights-out, and sat up in shock.

My eyes fell on, “I will sprinkle you with water to cleanse you from your iniquity”.

I had imagined my life to be exemplary, but it would seem not. I had obviously been weighed in the balance and found wanting.

Despite my flippancy, this was a positive and very profound action. One might, in today’s parlance, say a wake-up call.

With the amazing love and compassion of God, nothing is left to chance. I asked myself, why was this “sprinkling” done twice? It was done for a very specific reason. I was being reminded forever that God, with his infinite love for us all, cleanses and forgives us, not just once, but time after time after time.

All our vicissitudes are known; all we need to do is to acknowledge them and ask for forgiveness. All very simple and wonderful.

"So far as the East is from the West, your sins are forgiven you!" The very promise of God.

Late I came, remembering,
Remembering the vineyard.
There, lately came the worker who
Served for just one hour.
Just one hour he laboured,
Laboured well for Me,
A life time lost, but just one hour
'Twas good enough for Me.

The Chalice

To complicate my life further and leave me very uneasy, a most beautiful and memorable incident occurred on my day off.

I was revelling in the mid-week time off, knowing that I need not rush, and musing over the thousand and one things I had to do when, again, I knew my life was to be changed forever.

Where the ceiling meets the wall, just above my dressing table came a soft little humming sound which drew my attention. It was directly in line with the bed.

As I watched the extraordinary phenomenon, a beam of silvery light about five inches in diameter gradually fell towards my bed. I registered this and pulled myself up in the bed; I was awestruck as, from the top of the beam a chalice slowly coalesced and started to glide down the beam.

I was hardly daring to breathe as this unworldly event was taking place.

As the chalice came nearer to me, I saw flowers in it, rather like anemones, spilling over the side. The chalice was chased and of a silvery-looking metal, as were the flowers. It was all so other-worldly and absorbed me so entirely that I felt no longer of this world.

As strangely as this all began, so very slowly it all melted away, and the room seemed empty. What did it all mean, I asked myself, when I began to recover.

The chalice, we as Christians associate with only one person and one event. I felt a weight of responsibility was being placed upon me and it was difficult to understand why I was being used. It was to be a very long time before I knew the answer.

Holy Land

We had promised ourselves that one day we would go to the Holy Land and do what every Christian should do, journey up to Jerusalem.

The time came and, as we drove into Jerusalem in the early evening sun, the walls had a golden glow, reminding us of the hymn.

We were thrilled to be there: it was the cosmopolitan city that we expected and which has always comprised a disparate mixture.

Large men rode on little donkeys alongside Western opulence, BMWs etc. There was the hustle and bustle, the olive trees and the Kidron Valley, so much to explore. Flocks of sheep and goats would appear from nowhere. It was a terrain that had remained unchanged for centuries. We did it all. The Dead Sea, Masada, the Negev, Jericho, Galilee; we sat alongside the Galilean Sea eating St Peter's fish. It was all fascinating and timeless. So many millions had done what we were now doing and were no doubt as intoxicated.

The most poignant moment for me was time spent at Gethsemane. It was spring time and Madonna lilies blossomed beneath gnarled olive trees. These ancient olives, no doubt were seedlings from those that Our Lord knew, and at the time of his agony.

Nearby is the beautiful Church of the Agony. On the outer portals is a telling sculpture of our Lord in his agony being comforted by an angel.

It was all very stark and memorable.

In contrast to all this and not far away is the commercialisation that exploits biblical stories to the full. We look beyond that and realise all too well that we do not need to come to Jerusalem to find Jesus.

Having done all that people do in the Holy Land, we made our way to Tel Aviv for our flight home. On our last night we walked along the sea shore to Jaffa and conjured up images of how it might have been two thousand years ago.

We bought some treasures from the zealous traders and reluctantly made our way back to the noise and lights of Tel Aviv. We were to have an early start to be at Ben Gurion airport by 6am.

We dressed appropriately for the flight and made our way to the lifts.

We called the lift and I put a foot inside, only to slip violently on solid wax polish left by the early cleaners.

I fell dramatically and hard, nothing to save me! As I lay on the floor, I feared that I had done serious damage to my left hip.

After my years of orthopaedic nursing, I knew only too well what I had done. Through my light dress, having eased my fingers under my thigh, I felt the dreaded tell-tale sign of crepitus - that is, bone grating on bone. In my anguish, I yelled

"Please God, don't let my leg be broken, don't let it be broken!", and then lay quietly. My husband looked stricken, but said, "Do you think you can stand up?"

Moments before, I knew that was an impossibility, but now, somehow, I knew that I could.

I had had visions of the plane going without me, and being left behind in Tel Aviv. An impossible thought. Vernon helped me up and I could stand, although in severe pain. A doctor friend on the trip examined me, and was sure I would be OK to fly.

In my desperate petition to God I had limited my request, that my leg be "not broken". I didn't think beyond that. What I didn't know was that I had badly bruised the sciatic nerve and I suffered the effect for two years.

Anyway, I could walk and go home, and although the painful hip made life difficult, it could have been so much worse. How thankful I was that my desperate call to the Lord was heard. As we are taught, "Ask in my name, and it shall be given to you."

Faith

It is all about faith. When my husband was terminally ill in hospital, my daughter and I were in the lift descending to the ground floor, when we were challenged by a young woman.

There she was, puffing away at a cigarette, smelling heavily of nicotine and weighing not much more than six stone.

“I’ve just left my daughter”, she said, “stupid cow, she’s taken an overdose and doesn’t know anything. They don’t think they can do anything for her.” We were taken completely unawares and felt desperately sorry for this poor little woman. What on earth could we do - or say?

I said, “We will pray for her and hope that she will get better.” It seemed so banal and I wondered if it would mean anything to her. The daughter was called Samantha.

We were distracted from our own depressing thoughts by the seriousness of this very young girl. As we left the lift, the young woman chased after us, grabbed my arm and said, “Do you mean it? Will you pray for her?”

We assured her that we would, trusting that all would be well. This is the faith that moves mountains, that this unknown person would believe us, absolute strangers, and derive comfort from the fact.

I trust that Samantha is alive and well and happy with the mother who clearly, dearly loved her.

As nurses we are often in that privileged and unique position of being the last person a dying patient talks to. We are placed in compromising positions at times, which we cannot avoid.

One of my patients, terminally ill, had some time previously had surgery to remove his prostate gland. Following surgery, he developed an infection which needed treatment with a potent antibiotic. The result was tragic. He had driven himself to the hospital and left his car in the car park ready for his return home.

The side-effects left him totally blind and very deaf. With a deaf-aid in each ear, he could hear. He stopped me on what was to be one of his last days and said, “Tell me, Sister, am I going to die?”

I said, “Well, yes, Mr. Jones, I think you are, but then, you have much more to look forward to than most of us.”

Somewhat surprised, he said, “What makes you say that?”

“Because when the time comes, you will be able to see and hear.”

He smiled and thanked me for what I had said, and died a happy man.

A fellow patient was also very ill and I had turned him onto his side to give him an injection in his buttock. As I finished and eased him onto his back, he looked at me with what I can only describe as a look of horror on his face. "You know, don't you?" he said.

"What on earth do you mean?" I asked.

The whole story tumbled out as he was shedding tears. This man was a very highly respected retired headmaster and looked very pitiful.

It seems that he had been brought up in an extremely strict household and had been kept on a very tight rein. Once breaking free of all that, he began working towards a teaching degree in London.

The inevitable happened; he did break free, and behaved as he shouldn't have done! As he put it, he "caught a dose". At that time, the treatment for sexually transmitted diseases was harsh and painful. In his case, he was left with a permanently scarred skin and numerous brown markings, particularly on his back. I had seen them!

What can be said to such a person at the end of his life? I reminded him of the thousands of children he had influenced during his long teaching career, how much he had been loved by them, and what they owed to him. "You will be remembered not for one little misdemeanour, but for a lifetime of giving." I reminded him too of God's mercy and total forgiveness. Oh dear, are any of us "scar-free"? We are certainly not fit to judge others. He had carried this burden all his life. It is a salutary thought that today such a miscreant can be given one pill or one injection, and not a trace left! Nobody will know!

So much for progress.

Edith

When my husband retired from the police force, he wanted to be independent and work for himself away from the all the restrictions of a semi-military organisation.

To his delight a friend was selling a shoe business and gave Vernon first option to buy it. As I took in the ramifications of this complete change in life, I secretly trusted that it would not involve me. I loathed commerce and didn't even like shopping, so I prayed that I was not to be involved. How wrong I was!

My damaged sciatic nerve was still a nuisance to me and I had to admit to myself that it took an effort of will to carry on nursing. Pushing a trolley was quite an effort.

Sitting quietly after my lunch break one day, I suddenly decided that there was no need for me to put up with this hassle; I would leave.

As a result of holiday entitlement I could leave in three weeks. How short-sighted and stupid I had been. I had unwittingly played right into Vernon's hand. I could help him with the business, and I had no excuse to offer; I was trapped.

As the weeks went by, Vernon was elated by his “freedom”, and my depression knew no depth, as I was doing what I hated. But I had promised to “honour and obey” and obeying was making me ill. I hadn’t the heart to tell him.

I had arrived on duty shortly before I resigned and found to my dismay that one of the patients was very distressed. We had a male Matron at the time. It would appear that he had done an early morning round of Sick Bay. The lady concerned was quite a severe arthritic, for which she needed powerful anti-inflammatories. The side-effects of these could build up and cause major problems, as had happened in her case. She had had little choice in her treatment; either almost complete immobilisation, or the pills.

She had accepted her painful, debilitating condition with stoicism and grace, and was a much-liked patient.

The morning that provoked me to much anger was the day he had done the early round. For some reason, beyond understanding, he had told Edith, among other things, that she was a coward. It had distressed her considerably, and for the first time ever, she was in tears.

The side-effect she was experiencing was internal bleeding, too widespread for any helpful treatment and she had little time left. Obviously she was on sedatives. I did my best to ensure that her remaining conscious hours would be not only relatively pain-free, but also that she had no more torment. At a time when she should have been peaceful and tranquil, she had been callously upset; I was very angry. I too was now in the dog house.

This episode in Edith's life is relevant because of what occurred a few weeks later.

Vernon was delighted to be his own boss and was so wrapped up in his new venture that he was blissfully unaware of my severe depression; even nursing my painful hip was better than this!

Not long before Edith's descent into serious illness, we took her for an outing!

It was all very much against the rules, but then, in the interest of all, rules are broken.

Edith was a committed spiritualist and, during conversations, had talked about this. She knew I was an absolute cynic, but nevertheless she was highly intelligent, and what she had to say was very interesting.

Reading the local "rag" I noticed that a world-famous spiritualist was coming to the De Montfort Hall in Leicester to put on a show. I told Edith about this and she said that she knew Gordon Higginson very well, so I suggested we could possibly give her a real treat and take her along.

We planned it all meticulously, my husband picked us up at a rendezvous, and off we went.

The hall was packed, and Edith really looked forward to a wonderful evening. It meant absolutely nothing to us; we were Philistines!

Nevertheless, the whole thing was completely fascinating, as local people were targeted in sensational ways. We hear of plants put in the audience, but it was quite clear that this didn't happen. The speaker was an attractive, beautifully spoken man, a delight to listen to.

At the end of it all, my husband smuggled Edith back home, and the Matron was none the wiser.

Edith died not long before I resigned.

I had left! And was steeped in misery. One evening I had been busying myself upstairs and came down to hear the news on TV. Vernon was busy with his clerical work as I turned the news on, only it wasn't the news, I was on the wrong channel.

Before leaping up to change it, I heard a recognisable voice talking to an audience. I instantly recognised the voice of Gordon Higginson. I was amazed at the coincidence of switching the set on and hearing this voice. So I listened.

Very soon, to my amazement, he started to say, "I have a lady here who has passed over recently, you will know who it is, because you were there, and there had been trouble. She is saying that you will know what happened, and you will remember this. She is saying 'I can see rows and rows of shoes, rows and rows of shoes.' She says to tell you not to worry; everything will come out alright for you!"

I was spellbound! No one in the hall responded, but I knew beyond any doubt that Edith knew of my misery and was talking to me.

Spiritualists never talk of death, but of "passing over". The chance of me coming into the sitting room and randomly switching on the TV at the exact time that Gordon Higginson was speaking was incomprehensible! It was all intended, but how? Was I being guided by some means beyond my control, that I was to be watching a programme I knew nothing about, nor where it was coming from, to ease my woefully troubled mind! And by my brave, courageous patient Edith.

How on earth are those in the "beyond" to know so much of our whereabouts, and what we are doing?

I sprang into action, I was completely energised. I wrote to my immediate boss, the Secretary Superintendent, fishing to see if there was any chance of future re-instatement.

Two days later he rang me back and I was to be re-instated on my own terms, to start as soon as I liked!

I was jubilant, but not so my husband.

The situation was soon amicably resolved, and he employed someone in my place.

Being still on this side of the great divide, I have no idea how, by the use of modern technology, Edith was able to contact me.

It is obvious that time does not stand still over there and the advanced intelligence, of which we on this side know nothing, is capable of much to influence us in our own mortal lives.

Edith's intervention in my life is something I shall always be grateful for; she was, and always will be, a true friend.

The Old Testament Again

Vernon's work ethos knew no bounds, and became a worry. Asked to do or help with anything, it was always a challenge and he could not say no! He had been having headaches which he visited the doctor about, and was told he had a sinus infection. The "sinus infection" stayed. He visited the surgery three times, and I found that that his blood pressure was never checked. Alongside this, I was begging him to cut down his workload - to no avail.

When he drove home one October evening, he fairly staggered into the house; I knew there was something seriously wrong. How he drove the car home I shall never know.

I managed to get him into a chair and take his jacket off. I propped his leaden legs up onto a pouffe. He looked terribly weary and, as his limited speech became slurred, I knew the worst. I could see with horror a blood vessel visibly pulsating above his left eye as he gradually lost use of his right side. It was a moment of dread, I knew that he was having a stroke, or in medical parlance, a cerebral haemorrhage.

I was alone, so quickly rang the surgery to obtain the emergency number.

It seemed an eternity before the emergency doctor rang, and when he did I was angered because he said that he was in the village but could not find our house; would I come and show him the way! There was a brightly lit pub nearby which he could have popped into; everyone knew where we lived.

I had to leave my now unconscious husband alone whilst I went to look for him!

When we arrived home, the doctor seemed surprised by the degree of illness and promptly rang for an ambulance.

I was glad to see him go and leave me to gather some of Vernon's necessary equipment for his hospital stay.

Vernon's treasured ridgeback dog Jacob looked and howled miserably almost as if he were aware of the traumatic happenings.

None of the family was anywhere near, the nearest being John who was out for the evening; I left him a message on the answer phone.

Soon after our arrival at the hospital, John appeared, much to my relief. He looked shocked to see his father so ill.

With very few preliminaries, Vernon was taken straight to a medical ward and we were relieved to see him safely in bed and in care.

We were advised not to stay, as we could do little of use, and so we left the staff to their duties.

John and I were both in shock, and we arrived home at about 3am and he left for his home.

I took Jacob onto the back lawn as compensation for the evening walk he had missed and it seemed that the noble animal knew what was happening. I was thankful for his faithful companionship.

I went to bed, or rather to the bedroom, and spent much time on my knees. I knew only too well the consequences if the bleeding did not stop.

The thought of paralysis horrified me as he suffered a slight limp on his left side, a legacy from his earlier polio.

For the next breath-holding days nothing changed very much. I was spending my time dealing with the phone, visiting the hospital, walking Jacob and praying for a miracle.

One morning I was preoccupied in the kitchen, far away in my thoughts, when the grandfather clock in the living room struck nine. For some inexplicable reason I found myself walking into the room to view the clock! How crazy, the hands of the clock were on ten. Was I going mad? I went round checking the other clocks to see if it was nine or ten o'clock. It was only nine. So I had to open the clock case and hold the pendulum still to stop it and restart after an hour.

How stupid, I thought, as if I hadn't enough to cope with, this two hundred year old family clock deciding to be awkward at a time like this. I was irritated by the incident.

Anyway, the day progressed much as usual and Vernon's condition had stabilised; there appeared to be no more bleeding, and I dared to hope that the worst was over.

The morning after the clock incident, I was again busy in the kitchen when the chiming of the clock at nine jolted my memory about yesterday. Again I found myself wandering into the room to look at it.

I stood rooted to the spot. Again, the hands had advanced an hour to read ten o'clock!

I more or less fell onto the nearby settee and Jacob came and sat at my feet. I roused myself to open the case again and stop the pendulum.

I felt positively weak, and realised I was being told something.

Vernon had shown slight improvement, and had been playing up wanting to come home. For the reason of keeping him quiet, he was relegated to a side ward.

I began to breathe a little easier and dared to hope that he might get better.

That night, feeling more relaxed, I picked up my Bible from the bedside table and opened it at random. It told the story in the second book of Kings about King Hezekiah's sickness.

This very good king was, as it said, "sick unto death." He prayed fervently to the Lord, reminding him that he had always lived a righteous life. Having heard Hezekiah's supplications, the Lord spoke to the prophet Isaiah. "Tell Hezekiah I will heal him, and the sign will be that the shadow on the dial will go down ten degrees." Hezekiah, on hearing this, said, "It is an easy thing for the shadow to go down ten degrees, rather let it go up ten degrees." It happened as Hezekiah suggested: the shadow on the dial went forward ten degrees. Hezekiah was healed and reigned for another fifteen years. 2 Kings 20 9-11 KJV

I was spellbound as I read this. I was ignorant of the story before. Our old family clock was not as the "shadow on the step" of the Old Testament, but a more modern equivalent. The hands on our clock had moved forward a comparative one hour!

The movement of the clock hands had occurred twice to truly register it on my mind; it did not happen again. Was it possible, dare I hope that, like Hezekiah, Vernon would recover?

The truth is that Vernon was home, driving the car and running his business within three weeks.

We Lose Jacob

One of the most ghastly and saddest days of Vernon's life was a Monday. The usual practice was that he would be first in the kitchen in the morning to greet Jacob and bring him in.

This day the usual joyful bound did not occur. Only owners of the wonderful South African dog will know of the unique bond between dog and master, and the devastation of parting.

Jacob sat in his huge bed panting for breath and looking quite pitiful. We managed to get him onto a blanket and take him into the sitting room. As Vernon wept and tried to comfort Jacob, I sent for the vet who, mercifully, was with us in ten minutes. I knew beyond any doubt that Jacob had had a massive heart attack. As soon as the vet arrived our fears were confirmed and, being very used to the situation, as gently as he could, he advised that the kindest thing would be an injection to put Jacob to sleep. Vernon cradled him as he died and we were very thankful to have had these last moments with our truly loyal and magnificent treasure.

Life would never be quite the same for Vernon, although he maintained that I was number one for Jacob. Be that as it may, we were all decimated by the loss. Most probably , our beloved grand-daughter Becky, who suffers from cerebral palsy and is wheelchair bound. She loved him beyond knowing. When she was ill, he would sit by her bed and keep watch, and when she was well, would follow her about.

Jacob had been wonderfully cared for by our vet.

Thankfully, Easter was coming up and Vernon was kept well-occupied with his business, for which I was much gratified, as I could be of no comfort to him. On Maundy Thursday we went to a morning mass and the rest of the week passed for me in a haze.

On Easter Monday, I woke and realised there was no need to rush, and thankfully Vernon was fast asleep.

I was wondering what on earth we would do to fill the day, when my attention was drawn to an area just above my dressing table.

There, suspended in mid-air, or so it seemed, was Jacob in all the splendour of his young years. I looked at him in wonderment and said, “Oh Jacob, you’ve come back!”

As I said this, he gave me a quizzical look, tossed his head, as he would, and disappeared.

I sat dumb-struck. Vernon still slept on, so what was I to do? I needed to think. I slipped out of bed and went into the kitchen to make tea.

Would it be a good idea to tell Vernon or not? Would it upset him too much? After much thought, I decided to tell him.

I took the tea into the bedroom, sat on the bed and woke him up. Tears streamed down his face as I recounted exactly what had happened; it was all excruciatingly sad. When I had finished what I had to say, I was in for another shock.

Tearfully, he explained that when we were in church on Maundy Thursday, his last prayer to God was to plead that he may see Jacob just once more. I knew nothing of this, and was desperately sorry that Vernon did not see Jacob.

I now understand that those more spiritually aware are madeso by virtue of the pineal gland at the base of the skull. Perhaps that is why I was used.

It was an amazing happening, involving one of the animal world, but it reinforces the fact that this generation imagines itself advanced and informed, but much is not known and is certainly hidden from the doubters. We are all God's creatures, man and beast, and all are treasured.

Keys

A series of events suddenly occurred which mystified me, involving keys. To start with I decided that these incidents, many of them trivial, were due to carelessness on someone's part. So I ignored them until more positive incidents couldn't be treated as of no consequence.

I had bought myself a new jacket, but as usual the sleeves were too long, my arms being shorter than normal. So one evening I sat myself down and did the necessary alterations and put the jacket on a hanger in the hall.

The next day my priestly cousin and his wife were visiting us. As I walked through the hall that morning I glanced at a jacket of mine and on impulse took it and put it away in the larger of two wardrobes in the spare room. I turned the key and as I did so it flew out of my hand and I went to pick it up. It wasn't there. I had a cursory look round, couldn't see it, so decided I would come back later.

The jacket involved was quite expensive-looking, so the reason I moved it was because I felt it might look extravagant to my impoverished cousin on a priest's stipend.

Later in the day I remembered I had left the wardrobe key on the floor, so went to pick it up. It wasn't there. It was nowhere to be found, and I was irritated by this farcical situation.

The wardrobe was locked, and the rather heavy key had vanished. I decided I would blitz the bedroom and find the key. This I did meticulously, and the key was nowhere. I even stripped the beds, feeling rather ridiculous; the key had to be found. The key in the smaller wardrobe did not fit.

The next morning, before I did anything else, I tried on my new jacket (as my others were locked away!) and now it was okay, so I locked it in the smaller wardrobe.

On the following Sunday morning, Vernon had already driven the car down the drive ready for church and was waiting for me to join him.

As it was, it was rather chilly and I decided I needed a jacket, what better than my new one?

I unlocked the door, lifted the jacket off the rail and as I moved it, a clang sounded as the jacket hit the wardrobe door. Something heavy in one of the pockets. To my astonishment, it was the key of the large wardrobe - the missing key!

This jacket had been hanging in the hall when the key vanished, and now here the key was in the pocket. So where had the key been and how did it get inside the pocket of another jacket in the smaller wardrobe? No one had been near the room during this time!

A second interesting event took place when we were both going out to visit friends.

Again Vernon had driven the car onto the drive as I bolted the side gate, locked the outer kitchen door of the porch and the inner door to the kitchen. I put the keys, as we usually did, on the fridge. I glanced through the windows to check that Vernon was in the car and then crossed the kitchen, closing the door behind me. I crossed the living room into the hall and closed the hall door behind me. I walked the length of the hall and locked the inner and outer doors and left. It was a warm balmy evening and off we went.

We returned home at about eleven o'clock and followed our usual practice. Vernon garaged the car and would enter via the side garage door into the kitchen. I unlocked the front doors and as I walked down the hall felt a decided chill in the air. All the doors from the hall to the kitchen and porch were open to the elements and the keys still on the fridge. From the back, the house was kept safe by the side gate and garden gate – but what on earth was happening?

I had to accept that all the incidents were planned and meant to tell me something.

I puzzled over it all and finally, again feeling somewhat stupid, looked up "keys" in my concordance in a search for clues. The answer came and, as I accepted it, all the party games with keys stopped. "Peter, the rock on which I will build my church." Matthew 16 What did it all mean, and what was I to do? I had to accept that Jesus designated Peter as the head of His Church. As an Anglo-Catholic, was I being nudged in the direction of Rome, or was I to learn of the essential differences? I studied the different dogmas, the history of successive Popes and the great gulf between the various denominations, all very unsettling and disturbing. I had a feeling of unease.

The answer came in the small hours of the night, out of the blue, and produced much disturbance within me. This little village maid had come a long way. In the hush of the night a great truth was shared with me. "God had not wanted His church to be divided."

A little while elapsed before the connection between the vision of the chalice and the message of the keys was made plain to me.

The True Communion

We had gone to the ten o'clock communion service as was usual, but this day it was all to be very different.

We had not long had a new priest who proved to be very controversial. This church was fairly "high", but the new priest left beautiful vestments in the vestry, wearing only a surplice and scarf. The gospel procession was stopped and altogether we were in a state of schism!

My husband, who was on the PCC, rebelled against all this change and it resulted in the family decamping to another church, in fact a very beautiful church where his family had worshipped when he was a young boy.

But this day, the service had proceeded as usual and we were kneeling at the altar after the consecration. Suddenly the solemnity was shattered by a crash; the priest had dropped the paten. I opened my eyes at this point, and on the blue carpet the wafers shone like tiny stars, and I watched as the priest gathered them up and replaced them on the patten he was holding.

He then reconsecrated, but to my astonishment he was elevating the chalice and reconsecrating the wine. Oh dear, I thought, another mistake! But, how wrong I was!

As we arrived at home and left the car, I said, “That was pretty awful when Roy dropped the bread!”

Isabel and Vernon looked at each other and chorused, “Don’t be stupid, it was the wine he spilt!”

I said, “No, it was the bread; I saw it on the blue carpet”.

“You must have seen the wine on the carpet, and the staining on his surplice!” they said.

This I did not see. I saw no stain on the priest because I saw no stain in him. His wife had died not long before he came to us and I felt sorry for this lonely man.

The truth of the matter was that I saw something the others did not, and for a very specific reason. All my spiritual experiences culminated in this very direct lesson I was being taught.

Before this, we had invited a priest to the house to share a meal with us. He passed through my sitting room and noticed a photo of a robed priest.

He asked who it was and I explained and that it was taken on his ordination day in Winchester Cathedral. “Not a real priest”, was the comment. I was incensed at this remark, as I knew how dedicated this priest and his wife are to their community. But this man is not alone in this view.

I had had a great truth shared with me that "God had not wanted His Church to be divided." Jesus said, "A house divided against itself will fall", so division weakens - Jesus said so!

With division there are those who fail to believe the very words of Christ: "This is my body, this is my blood" at the Communion rail.

So the vision I saw of the "blood" changed to bread was to teach me a great truth.

In that Anglican Church, with an Anglican priest, Christ was present. Only He could have changed in front of my eyes, the wine for bread.

The proof of the presence of Our Lord at that Anglican service on that Sunday morning was absolute. Those that do not accept this truth are questioning the very words of Christ and the reason for His death.

When I went to Leicester to start my four year course of General Training, I was shocked on Good Friday to see the market stalls erected and trading going on. Trams were running and shops were open on this most Holy day.

And what of the Sabbath, so much allowed and accepted!

Are we truly to believe that we of the present age have the authority to question our Commandments?

When King David was bringing up the Ark of the Covenant to Jerusalem on a cart, a bullock cart, at one point the vehicle shook. One of the assembly put his hand onto the Ark to steady it.

He was not a priest. The Lord was so angered that Uzziah was smitten and died. II Samuel 6.

This is a small example of the sanctity with which God expected His Word to be treated. With great reverence. I must say that I found this salutary lesson showing the truth of Anglican Orders very uplifting.

I had long thought that when a Bishop presents an ordinand for the priesthood it is not the bishop, be he Anglican or Roman, it is not him that ordains, but Our Lord. So, in the eyes of God, the ordinands are of equal worth.

Faith

Thoughts transmit to the world beyond as our prayers do. Chaos would ensue if all our prayers were to be answered as we would like; there would be no room for any of us!

We are given free will to do with our bodies what we will; it is no good overeating, drinking too much, exposing ourselves to too much radiation and expecting God to "rub it out!" God is not a bottle of medicine to be thought about and reached for when things go wrong. Are we to believe that if we have faith of the right sort we can affect the mind of God? If someone dear to us is mangled in a dreadful car accident, that God will put it right? Should we blame God if the dearly loved one dies?

We cannot use faith to manipulate God, but faith in God will allow us to accept His will.

My strange and unique spiritual experiences bear out the truth of God's promises to us in the Old Testament. Remarkable events did not just happen 2,000 years or more ago; they are continuous, but God will not be mocked. I have learned during my lifetime that God is a hard taskmaster and expects obedience to his will, nothing diluted.

To become a good golfer or tennis player, commitment is needed, and so it is with faith.

If we put nothing in, we can expect nothing.

I have been graphically shown that we do survive death of the body.

When we are very young we have no idea what pain is, what a headache is, or what it is to be “good”. As we journey through life, we develop our spiritual selves and the indestructible soul. The spirit or soul, cannot be destroyed by any human entity, nor can anything be erased.

Jesus has promised us that we shall be invested, on death, with the spiritual garment that we deserve. Just before my mother died, she had a vision which she shared with my grieving father.

“There are thousands and thousands there, Arthur. And I have qualified, and I don’t want to be disqualified.”

Would that we all might be so blessed.

The little pile of ash, or the body left behind, does not hold our imprint that has already gone.

More Inhumanity To Man

During my many astounding spiritual encounters, it has been proved to me that not only are we known in the world beyond, but it seems our paths are known before we are aware of what is happening; "they" are in front of us! Remember the incident involving my expensive jacket hanging in the hall? The bizarre events that followed had been planned before I knew of them. It was known that morning how I was going to think! That would seem to be the answer, but more intriguingly, was the thought put in my mind in order to facilitate the train of events that followed?

More mysterious was my spiritualist friend who knew of my distress, acted on it, and contacted me via the television, to my great relief.

Doubters must remember that events recorded in the Bible were strange; seemingly impossible incidents occurred. It must be known that great forces of which we make use exist even though we cannot see them (for example gravity and radiation), yet we accept them. And yet the greatest of all forces, for some unfathomable reason, is shown to some of us in a physical or metaphysical way.

For all Christian people, the way to God is by way of Jesus, our Paraclete. Others have different advocates which we must accept; they, like us, are striving towards their final destination.

We all accept without question that the Angel Gabriel appeared to Mary to announce her forthcoming motherhood and the birth of Jesus. There can only be one Angel Gabriel, and Muslims believe that he instructed Mohammed in their faith.

St Paul, our great teacher, was an enemy of Jesus, and only "knew" the Risen Lord after his dramatic experience on the way to Damascus. So why was he so very knowledgeable? It proves the truth of the blessed Holy Spirit; also that many others have been so blessed. We must not have closed minds.

None of we mortals have been to the Holy Places and come back, so we are in no position to doubt, or question what has happened to others.

It is sad that we have so many empty churches. Today people think, and are better informed with "knowledge" they acquire from the internet, so they will not be told what to think; they question everything. Also, so many feel that they have no need of God! A situation that causes problems is that of homosexuality. It is all very open today, and much talked about. It is only of comparatively recent years that it is known that an area of the brain differs slightly according to our sexuality.

There are known small areas that are structurally modified and inbuilt.

We are born with random appurtenances for which we are not responsible, they are part of us. But we are responsible for how we treat and judge others we consider different. I have spent the best years of my life caring for the sick and suffering, and I find the setting-aside of these people, or any, for different reasons, quite cruel. It is a case of, "there but for the grace of God go I." We are all God's creatures, none of us of greater worth or special.

Many people claim that they have been contacted and spoken to by Jesus with life-changing results, but have to accept that they are considered by many to be cranks. The name-callers who take that attitude must remember that God will not be mocked, and they are less likely to receive comfort or help themselves.

It is easy to become cynical in this materialistic and shallow age, but the world is full of caring folk.

Goodness is not news, nor are the virtues of love, faith, wisdom and modesty, but they are worth striving for. It would seem that when Our Lord walked in Galilee, his life was very simple and he showed a great love and interest in the simple loveliness of things not made with hands; those things which cost nothing are for all to share. He spoke of the animals, the sheep, the goats, the trees and the wind, listing where it will. The sparrows, "four for a farthing", but perhaps the loveliest of all are his thoughts about the flowers. "Behold the lilies of the field, they toil not, neither do they spin." So sublime.

How carelessly we take nature's bounty for granted and hardly notice it, it being lost to so much artificiality and materialism.

Can man, clever as he is, go into a laboratory and make a primrose and, having done that, infuse it with its delicate perfume?

We are living in an age when the church is under severe attack, and unfortunately the non-believers make much noise and are given a lot of space. Those of us that are believers and "walk in the light" must make our voice heard, remembering that it is our duty.

We are continually being told that our country is one of the richest in the world.

We have wealth, expertise and knowledge - but have we found Nirvana?

I have written my story in the full knowledge that I shall have to give account of myself on my last day, so I would be nothing short of a fool to have written anything not scrupulously truthful. For reasons that may eventually be shown to me, I have been used as a conduit to help those in any doubt to know the love of God and the truth of His promises to us.

I am one of the least in this world, but am emboldened to write my story, remembering the words of the Decembrist, the Russian diplomat Konstantin Aksakov who wrote:

"The lone voice is a moral choir, in which one voice is not lost, but heard in the harmony of all voices."

Vernon

One day I was much surprised when Vernon suddenly said to me, "You will never leave me, will you, I couldn't live without you." I was completely taken aback. I said, "Don't be silly, of course you will live, the children will need you. They need us just as much now as when they were little."

How trite and easily said that was within the security of marriage, but how difficult the reality became a few months later, when I was the one to be left.

Vernon began to show symptoms of a minor heart problem, which meant visits to the surgery. The condition was easily contained and Vernon had returned to all his normal activities. However, one day the doctor suggested, just to be on the safe side, that he should see a consultant.

This duly followed. The consultant was a cheerful fellow, and Vernon instantly liked him, trusted him and was sure he would soon sort him out.

I sat in the room and heard him say, "I must get that blood pressure down" after checking Vernon. I was astonished and said, "Vernon's blood pressure has been within normal limits for years, without any medication."

"Nonetheless, the blood pressure has got to come down below normal limits."

I was very troubled at this, as I said that I had twice had to take Vernon back to surgery when he reacted very badly to blood pressure tablets. I stressed that he had been made very ill, and worryingly so. I was totally disregarded, and Vernon accepted two lots of blood pressure pills, to work in tandem.

My heart sank to my boots. I was very worried about this turn of events. It seemed this Consultant had decided there and then that Vernon should see a surgeon with a view to surgery. Again, the whole family found this very concerning.

Having spent my years nursing, and with my early indoctrination on professional ethics including treating consultants like gods and never, never questioning their word, I found it hard to challenge this man.

It wasn't long before Vernon began to go downhill, sleeping 18 hours daily, falling and eventually developing a sore toe. The next visit to the consultant was not at all comforting, as I explained that Vernon's heart condition seemed to be getting worse. "Nothing to do with the heart condition," he said, "all to do with my medication. Reduce the pills by half."

The damage was done, and Vernon's toes began to go black, and infarcts, clots, formed in his brain. "Too widespread." a very kind neurologist told me, "Too widespread for any treatment. Your husband might live for two years, but could be dead in six months."

My worst day of all was the day a bright young nurse met me as I was visiting and said, "Your husband has been eating the plant today, on the table in front of him." It was like an arrow hitting me, but it said it all - Vernon did not know who he was, where he was, and much of the time he didn't seem to know who we were.

He lived in this state for nine months.

Our son, a priest, preached at his requiem mass and Vernon was much honoured. He had a number special to him. Strangely, his treasured Ridgeback, Jacob, had died exactly seven years before, on the same day, March 28th.

My sorrow was put to good effect. Within the state of marriage, its protection, security and sanctity, a feeling of invincibility ensues. It is never going to end or change! When change comes suddenly, cruelly, it is like a heavy dose of poison that leaves one rudderless, helpless and afraid.

We all have to die, but the manner of Vernon's death was painful and cruel not only to him but to all who loved him. He had been a very intelligent, sensitive and hard-working man, working hard especially for the children that he loved.

I felt I should have prevented all that happened to him, had I had the courage to have been more outspoken to the consultant! The lesson learned is that no matter how elevated a person is, mistakes are made! When in doubt, a second opinion should be sought, as I have learned to my cost.

My abject feelings of guilt and inadequacy forced me into a pit of deep despair and I felt utter disgust with myself. I had cared so much for others but could do nothing for my husband. I was in a bottomless pit and also felt abandoned by God.

During this time, I read the book written by Dietrich Bonhoeffer, the German martyr. He was alleged to be part of a plot to kill Hitler, and was imprisoned awaiting execution. A Lutheran Pastor, engaged to be married, his position was dire.

In his book written in prison he quotes from Adalbert Stifter. “Pain is a Holy Angel who shows to us treasures which would otherwise remain forever hidden. Through him we have become greater than through all the joys of the world.” It would seem that Bonhoeffer found much comfort in these lines, which express a profound truth. It took me a very long time to accept these noble sentiments and feel shame for my own self-pity.

I realised that all my anger and blame was misplaced and I was truly humbled.

Vernon was a non-confrontational person and would have laid no blame on the doctor, whom he liked. He never looked for, nor sought fault in any one.

We of faith believe that this life is a proving ground; we all have free will to live a life caring for others, or otherwise - the choice is ours.

I believe we are judged by our acceptance of adversity. Vernon accepted his adversity, never once complained during this time of preparation for the "Greater Light" that he was to enter.

Vernon was prepared for the "Greater Light"; I was not. I had much amending to do, but over time gradually I felt I had been gathered up and forgiven.

A blind priest and poet of long ago, one George Matheson wrote:

"Lord, I have thanked thee for my roses, but never for my thorns."

I now felt at long last that I too could thank God for my "thorns".

Love Story

A shy young man was admitted to the medical ward I was nursing on. I had little contact with him as he was not on my list of patients.

He had polio. As he began to recover and move up the ward(the more poorly patients would occupy the beds nearest the door – known as 'Gabriels Corner'), he would give me a grin and offer me a sweet, usually Cadbury's Roses. I paid little attention to him. At the time I was in my third year of General Training and had two stripes on my shoulders.

After his discharge he would wander up to the ward after attending Outpatients.

It suddenly dawned on me that I was the object of this attention. I was somewhat embarrassed by this, as nurses in training were strictly not to fraternize with patients.

Rules disregarded, it wasn't long before, as they say today, we were "an item".

One night at the "flicks" an arm suddenly shot round my shoulder in a warm embrace.

"Oh dear", I thought, "this is progressing too fast!"

I was at the stage of studying hard for my hospital exams and state finals, so I had to tell him that the association had to stop. I hated doing this to him, but I settled down to my studies and passed my exams with flying colours.

About eighteen months later I had a very vivid dream, right out of the blue, and the dream I had was of the polio patient – Vernon.

I was now a Charge Nurse and I suppose feeling my feet a little, with my frilly goffered lace cap and navy blue uniform.

The vivid dream recurred several times and was imprinted on my mind. So I wrote to Vernon. Little did I know that by now he was in the army, in the Middle East, in the Canal Zone. His mother obviously forwarded my letter to him and I was replied to. Our courtship, which is what it now was, continued apace.

When he came home, he showered me with presents, some of which I felt should have been for his mother as he was an only child.

Among my gifts was a beautiful white silk under-slip which I thought rather bold and presumptuous of him! How innocent we were in those days.

He proposed to me, on his knees, in Hubbard's Hills, a beauty spot in Lincolnshire. He took me out to the "Forest" in Leicestershire to give me my engagement ring on my birthday. He was so nervous he had a nose bleed.

Only those that have shared great happiness over long years will know the devastation of parting.

I was as one teetering over an abyss. There was a pulling towards, a drawing towards and a yearning to be on that "other side", with the half of me already there.

Only willpower, duty and the devotion of the children drew me back home to them.

Beloved

Meeting in the Springtime, we shared our Salad days
Our thoughts were not of years ahead
Were blind to life's hard ways
Ill prepared for tempests that would test our Wonderland
We learned from one another of life
that was not planned.

You built for me a Taj Mahal and furnished it with love
There to spend our Golden days when labouring was done.
We joyed to watch the wild life,
The swallows skim the pond,
We listened to the plaintive call of straying sheep and lambs
The clip-clop of the horses and the pealing of the bells
To call to mind our transience,
So treasur'd time we'd spend.

We in our folly had planned the time ahead

But others in a far-off land knew of our fantasies.

They thought not to tell us, or think to change their mind

They came and took you silently

Unseen, unknown, alone.

Margaret

ND - #0256 - 080726 - C0 - 197/132/10 - PB - 9781780352862 - Gloss Lamination